SAY IT STRAIGHT
Or You'll Show It Crooked

ABE WAGNER

T.A. COMMUNICATIONS, INC.

This book is available at a special discount when ordered in large quantities. Contact T.A. Communications, Inc., 10200 E. Girard Avenue, #B-230, Denver, CO 80231.

Contact Abe Wagner & Associates.
Published in 1998 by T.A. Communications, Inc.

Edited and published in 1992 by T.A. Communications, Inc.
10200 E. Girard Avenue, #B-230, Denver, CO 80231 USA

First edition, 1986

Translations
Japanese (Japan UNI Agency, Inc., 1990)
ISBN 4-390-60340-X C0011 P1600E

Spanish (Grijalbo, 1991)
ISBN 970-05-0196-5

The Industrial Society 1996
Robert Hyde House
48 Bryanston Square
London W1H 7LN

ISBN 1 85835 402 1

British Library Cataloguing-in-Publication Data.
A Catalogue record for this book is available from the British Library.

CONTENTS

CONTENTS

ACKNOWLEDGEMENTS

How do I thank the many people who helped me to write this book? The simplest way is to simply say a heartfelt *'thanks'*. Thanks to my son Doug for allowing me to practice my ideas with him. Thanks to my sons, Daniel and David, and my sister Rosalie, for their fine job of initial editing. Final editing of this book was assisted by Julie Evans, who has a keen eye for language use and excellent computer skills. Susan Rae Friedman (I'm her husband), invested a great deal of time and energy transforming an okay book into an excellent book. She is a continual source of intellectual stimulation, caring and love.

Lastly, I want to thank my father, Harry Wagner, who provided an extremely important role model for me as a youngster. He was the kind of individual who lived the vast majority of the 'Say It Straight' principles. He was a man who devoted his life to others. Even though my father passed away when I was very young, I shall always love him. His love and guidance remain with me today.

SAY IT STRAIGHT PRINCIPLES

1. Say it straight or you'll show it crooked.

2. Direct your activity to accomplish goals.

3. Treat yourself and others with dignity and respect.

4. Be self-determining and help others to do the same.

5. Be responsible for your own thinking, feeling and behavior.

6. Live in the here and now.

7. Resolve issues rather than being right.

8. Continue what works, change what doesn't work.

9. Ask for what you want and ask others to do the same.

10. Make agreements that you are willing and intend to keep.

11. Appropriately involve others in making decisions that affect them.

12. Give and accept positive strokes and feedback.

13. Express your feelings appropriately.

14. Communicate with people who can help resolve conflict.

foreword

Say it straight or you'll show it crooked

When Abe Wagner asked me to write the foreword for this book, I was very pleased. I have known Abe for ten years now and feel he is one of the best communicators I know. He has the uncanny capacity to take complicated concepts and make them easily understood by everyone. *SAY IT STRAIGHT Or You'll Show It Crooked* is a beautiful example of this wonderful skill.

This is an honest, caring book about achieving better communication and stronger relationships with those people who are important in your life. It builds on Abe's earlier work, *THE TRANSACTIONAL MANAGER*, and seeks to offer a handful of guiding principles for building cooperation and respect with others. These principles are, in some cases, well founded, and in others, relatively new. Yet, in each case, Abe has thoroughly shown the importance of the concept and offered many suggestions for how it can be achieved. Examples, including ones from his own life, are frequent. The book is vintage Abe Wagner.

From how to take control of one's own life to how to communicate in a sensitive, caring manner, Abe has systematically outlined many simple methods for keeping relationships on an equal footing. Some are commonly overlooked and others have slipped away because we have tended to take them for granted in our relationships.

SAY IT STRAIGHT Or You'll Show It Crooked reaffirms such valuable concepts as that of 'unconditional positive regard', which I feel is a critical foundation for both managers and parents to establish with the group of individuals with whom they primarily interact.

I think you are really going to like this book and are going to find it helpful in your everyday interaction with others. Enjoy and use the concepts. Let Abe Wagner be your guide to increasing your communication effectiveness.

Kenneth Blanchard, Ph. D.
Co-author, *THE ONE-MINUTE MANAGER*

introduction

My personal and professional life experiences have
led me to the conclusion that there are certain basic
concepts and principles by which individuals,
groups, organizations — yes, governments — could live
that would result in real happiness and prosperity.
Many people, families and organizations do live very
successfully by their own modified versions of the
concepts in *Say It Straight.* As I live my life using these
ideas, I become more and more convinced of their virtue
and broad applicability, in both personal and
professional relationships.

I went to a seminar several years ago. The leader of
this workshop had made several million dollars in a
relatively short period of time. He had formed a new
company, one that began by remodelling Victorian homes
in the Bay area of California. The unusual thing about
this company was that the president purposely set out
to make sure that the members of the organization lived
by some basic, simple rules concerning their
relationships with one another. He wondered whether
some of the 'corny' ideas prevalent in the field of
humanistic psychology could really be employed in the
'dog-eat-dog' business world. He found that they
certainly could. His success was astounding.

It is in part from that humanistic approach that the
Say It Straight guidelines evolved. They are common
sense ideas which can be learned and put into practice
with relative ease. They are as effective and relevant for
an interpersonal relationship between two, as for a
professional organization of two thousand.

The *Say It Straight* model provides a simple
framework for obtaining cooperation, communicating
clearly, and conveying a genuine sense of respect for

others. Even if one person in an organization or group starts using these principles, improvements will begin. For best results, however, they should be practiced by all. Present members can be asked to agree to follow these guidelines, with the assurance that, by doing so, they will receive support from the top. Prospective employees can be asked to read the principles and agree to follow them when hired. Once the members of an organization have accepted these concepts, it is up to the leaders, as well as all participants, to strive for their consistent implementation. The content of the principles enclosed in this book may be used as a simple checklist for evaluating a person's 'people skills', as well as a problem-solving tool when difficulties in communication arise.

One other element of this book to which I wish to make reference is my desire to inject humor when it's appropriate. I plan to share with you a few of my favorite stories, thereby giving the intellectual part of you a rest, and letting the playful part of you have a little fun. The added benefit to you is that when you laugh, you actually help yourself to physically fight off illness, and promote a sense of well-being. *Humor is depicted in italics herein, thus you'll know when to laugh.*

1 say it straight or you'll show it crooked

Say it straight has many meanings

What does 'Say It Straight Or You'll Show It Crooked' mean? In essence, it means that if I have a strong feeling or a desire, and I don't do something effective about it, I will end up, internally or externally, somehow demonstrating that feeling or desire in an ineffective manner. For example, if I'm angry with someone, and I don't tell him that I'm irritated and what I'm irritated about, it's likely that I will consciously or subconsciously express my anger in another way. I may forget to do what he wanted me to do, do it wrong, procrastinate, do it late, talk about him behind his back, 'accidentally' do him harm, take my anger out on somebody else, overeat, smoke, get depressed, worry, become agitated, have sleepless nights. That's the nature of the beast. Unexpressed negative feelings and unfulfilled desires get acted out in ways that are inappropriate if we don't express or act on them in ways that are appropriate.

'Say It Straight' does not always have to involve sharing your feelings, thoughts, and desires with someone else, especially when the other person will react negatively to you for doing so, or is clearly unwilling to respond as you would like, or is not available to communicate with you. It is necessary, however, to admit your feelings to yourself, experience them, and utilize, in some positive way, the energy that those feelings generate for you. You can use the energy to resolve your feelings in a variety of ways. You may re-examine the situation, and gain a new understanding that would help you to solve the problem, or you may become content to simply drop your anger, fear or sadness. You may find some substitute way of getting what you want, or you may look elsewhere.

Feelings left over after the situation has been handled as well as possible can be discharged through symbolic acts such as writing a letter and burning it, by hitting a mattress with an old tennis racket, or by yelling, crying, or screaming in a place where you will not be overheard — in your car, or in the shower. For example, I was talking to myself in the car one day, and continued talking while stopped at a traffic light. I was a bit uncomfortable when I looked up and saw people watching me. I rolled down the window and said, 'He's very small.' This is called the 'empty-chair technique', and will be discussed later. It can be useful as well.

Sensitive versus blatant honesty

Saying it straight means being sensitively, rather than blatantly honest. For example, *instead of saying, 'You're a liar,' it's better to say, 'Sometimes you really don't say it straight.'* It is possible to express feelings in a way that takes other people into consideration. I truly do unto others as I would have them do unto me. This is a guideline that works well for me because I like myself. It doesn't work so well for everybody, however, because some people don't like themselves and don't care how others treat them.

Before confronting someone in an honest fashion, I recommend asking, 'What is my purpose? What do I want to accomplish?' Often, the answers are, 'I want to feel better,' and/or, 'I would like them to understand my position.' Sometimes it is that I want them to change their behavior. Being aware of my goal helps me to communicate in a way that invites the appropriate outcome.

Before saying something that may be insensitive, ask yourself, 'Will I get a positive outcome by sharing this? Will it benefit me or the other person, or help to solve a problem?' If not, why share the information?

Some things, however, are better left unsaid. William Blake said, 'A truth told with bad intent is worse than any lie you can invent.'

It is possible to carry out confrontations without an attack on the individual's worth, motives, personality, race, sex or intelligence. Some people have as their motto, 'I call 'em as I see 'em.' Under the umbrella of honesty, they accuse, name-call, exaggerate, shout and attack people in front of others. They feel justified because they are 'being honest'. This approach seldom brings good results. *Confucius is reported to have said, 'He who slings mud loses ground.'* Focus instead on a factual description of the person's behavior. Avoid making interpretations about what motivated him, exaggerating what he did, or calling him names.

A friend of mine went out on a blind date one evening. I asked her how it went, and she replied, 'Well, he was a little strange. He hadn't talked to me in 45 minutes, and then he said, "I guess

*you've noticed that I've been very quiet. Let me
level with you. It's because I'm disappointed that
you're not very attractive.'"* This man certainly
scored high on the 'virtue' scale, if honesty is a
virtue. He flunked on the 'sensitivity' scale.

There is virtue and strength in saying what you think or
expressing how you feel. Many people short-change
themselves and others when they say nothing. When you
take that quality of openness and mix it with sensitivity,
you have a powerful combination. Many things are more
valuable in combination.

Sensitivity is necessary in determining not only whether
and how to say something, but also when and under what
circumstances to say it. Recently, a secretary said to her
boss, in front of many people, 'You made a mista-a-ake!'
She said this in a cute way, a friendly way, but the 'when'
and 'under what circumstances' were problems in this
particular confrontation. It is unwise to confront people at
a time when they will not be receptive. It is usually
irresponsible to confront people in front of third parties.
If you must make a choice between sensitivity and total
honesty, sensitivity is usually a higher value. Fortunately,
you and I are able to be sensitively honest under the vast
majority of circumstances.

I am not suggesting that you should never say things
about others that they might regard as uncomplimentary
or from which they might experience pain. I am
suggesting, however, that it is quite possible to ask for
behavioral change or provide feedback in a way that
invites listening instead of defensiveness or angry
responses. Specific ways to do that will be illustrated in
later chapters.

I will give one example here, however, of a way that I
once handled a difficult confrontation. Years ago I was
supervising a young European man whose body odor was
very offensive to his co-workers. I was asked to confront
him about this problem. I could have done so indirectly,
by putting a bar of deodorant soap on his desk, or some
anti – perspirant. I could have told him to have a shower,

'because you stink.' Instead, I decided to give him some information. I let him know that Americans had many idiosyncrasies and that we had unwritten standards about showering and deodorants. I told him I thought it would be to his advantage to be sensitive to these standards about deodorants and that by doing so he would enhance his working relationships. This was done gently and in a caring fashion. He responded very well to this approach.

The remainder of this book will provide operational how-to's for *Saying It Straight.* These are guidelines I have used in my own life, and firmly believe they have played a major role in both my professional success and personal growth. The most common problems within organizations are generally the result of a breakdown of one or more of the *Say It Straight* principles. Conversely, those organizations and groups which incorporate and adhere to these principles report a more efficient work environment, more productive and cooperative group members, a more relaxed atmosphere, greater loyalty, and a sense of enthusiasm and growth.

2 direct your activity to accomplish goals

This guideline applies not only to individuals, but also to groups such as departments, organizations, and families. Invite people to be definitive about their goals, and be definitive about your own.

This idea is as simple as knowing what results you want before you talk to someone. If, when confronting a person, you want him to change his behavior, then the method you choose will be designed to accomplish that goal. If, on the other hand, your purpose is simply to unload and feel better, you may speak in an entirely different way.

The mind is a goal-striving mechanism

The human mind is a goal-striving mechanism. We are similar to a self-guiding missile system on its way to a target. Our conscious and subconscious minds are geared to achieving goals and solving well-defined problems. When the missile veers off course, it corrects itself. Another interesting thing about the human mind is that it has a tendency to store successful experiences and to forget unsuccessful experiences once they have been corrected. Ultimately, the successful person is the one who establishes goals and meets them.

Having a clear definition of goals to be accomplished or problems to be solved is extremely important for their ultimate resolution. Many people resist defining goals because they have no idea how to accomplish them. The fascinating thing about the human mind is that when we do set a goal, the subconscious mind often tells and shows us how we're going to accomplish it. Those thoughts and ideas come to consciousness as we are ready for them. A wonderful example of this process is the flashes of insight that you and I have that are often extremely creative. For instance, what happens when you 'sleep on a problem' that you don't know how to solve? On a number of occasions, I have gone to sleep with a problem on my mind and have awakened with a solution, without consciously thinking about the problem at all.

Beliefs also become goals. People with negative beliefs about themselves end up demonstrating those beliefs. The person who believes that employers are not hiring will not be likely to get the job. He may go to the employment office poorly dressed and say something like, 'You're not hiring, are you?' He doesn't get hired but he was 'successful' because he achieved his 'goal'. Obviously, the key is to convert negative thoughts and ideas into positive thoughts and ideas.

One of the biggest problems existing within some organizations is the lack of clarity about goals. Individuals, departments, upper management, and sometimes entire organizations may be unclear about the goals for today, the goals for a given meeting or the organization's short and long-term goals. It follows that if people do not understand their goals, they are not directed in a very clear fashion. How can they then be evaluated about their performance if it is not based on some kind of mutually accepted and quantifiable goal?

Imagine going to a bowling alley that has a sheet hanging in front of the pins. You roll the ball down the alley, and it looks as though your ball is going to hit a strike. You hear the noise of the pins, but you have no idea how many you knocked down. How long will you bowl? What if you are told your score only once a year at your performance evaluation? And what if you then learn that you have been throwing gutter balls when you thought that you were throwing strikes and spares? Isn't that essentially the problem that people face when they can't see their goals and they don't know how they are doing in relation to them?

GOALS MUST BE QUANTIFIABLE AND PERSONALLY FULFILLING

The key issue is to have goals which are not only well-defined but are also quantifiable. This applies to both the individual and the organization. If I know how much work I want to complete, how many sales calls I want to make, how many units I want to sell, how much money I want to earn, how many customers I want to serve per hour or per day, I can measure my progress toward these goals. If I know what specific types of behavior I have to engage in to be an effective manager, then I'll know when I've achieved my goal.

The final key element is that goals must contain an element of personal desire. It is difficult to make yourself put a lot of energy into reaching a goal in which you are not personally invested. Have you ever tried to lose weight because somebody else thought that you were too heavy? Rarely is that sort of project successful. Start by answering this question: 'What's in it for me?'

The more specific the goal, the better. If you are talking about losing weight, how much weight? If you are talking about improving your ability to supervise, what specific behavior do you want to change? The more specific the goal is, the more quantifiable it becomes. For example, 'I'll meet him weekly, and I'll acknowledge that I understand, instead of countering with my own point of view.'

Relate the goals to accomplishing specific types of behavior or specific tasks, when this is appropriate. It is quite difficult to measure 'happiness', for example. On the other hand, if we knew what you would do differently when you were happy, we could measure that: 'When I am happy, I will weigh 150 pounds or less;' or, 'I will exercise for thirty minutes daily;' or, 'I will be with friends at least twice a week;' or, 'I will watch at least one sporting event weekly.' If my goal is to become a better parent, that goal needs definition, such as, 'I will spend one-to-one time with each of my children for at least one hour every week;' 'I will help my son with his homework when he asks;' 'I will become consistent in my expectations of my children;' 'I will practice what I preach.'

It is important to define quantity, if that is an issue. Often, people will set a goal that encompasses doing something more or something less. How much is 'more'? The more specific the quantity, the easier to measure your achievement.

Time allocations are sometimes appropriate. Having a specific time as part of the goal makes it much easier to measure, and often easier to accomplish. 'I will lose ten pounds by August 30th;' or, 'I'll save $50 a month.'

Also of value is building in short-term successes. Often people have a two-year goal, or a five-year goal, which is fine if they have opportunities to feel successful at points along the way. It is difficult to wait a long time to reach a goal because people lose interest. If my goal were to retire by the age of 55, given that I am now 45, I would have a ten-year goal. To reach that goal, and also to build-in short-term successes, I would want to determine not only how much money I would need to have saved at the end of those ten years, but also how much money I would need to save yearly, perhaps monthly. Then each month that I save the necessary amount, I feel good about my success. This helps me to stay motivated. I also recommend that people reward themselves when they have made a significant short-term achievement. Do something that is fun — such as see a good friend.

It is useful to put goals in positive, rather than negative terms. One key principle of psychology is that when you take away one kind of behavior you must replace it with something else. For example, if my goal is to stop being defensive when criticized by my employer, I will replace that behavior with actively listening to the feedback, making sure that I understand it, and then assessing its value as objectively as possible. Finally, I will

communicate to my employer my understanding of his or
her comments.

Another reason for using positive instead of negative
terms is that the subconscious mind takes a negative
comment as a directive. The subconscious mind does not
distinguish a 'do' from a 'don't'. Therefore, the message
'don't drink' is the same as 'drink'. If you wish to stop
smoking, then focus on fresh air. If you wish to stop being
intolerant of others, focus on listening and understanding
others. If you wish to stop being blatantly honest, then
concentrate on how you would look, sound, and feel if you
were sensitively honest.

If your goal is not in keeping with your own self-image,
you will find it very difficult to believe. However, many
people err in that they unnecessarily limit themselves.
Limitations are, by and large, self-imposed. People are
capable of much more than they believe. George Bernard
Shaw said that whatever the mind can conceive and
believe, you can achieve. There must still be some degree
of realism in the goal, or you won't believe it. Many people
strive for perfection, an unrealistic goal, rather than
excellence, which can be achieved. When you strive for
unrealistic goals, the end result is a great deal of
frustration, and a sense of failure.

The mind focuses on one target at a time much better
than several. One way to fail is to set too many goals.
Limit current goals to two or three, and then add more as
you accomplish the early ones. I remember the numbers of
people who came into psychotherapy and wanted to
change too many aspects of their behavior. *Then there was
the fellow with only one thing he wanted to change. He
came into a therapy session one day with a duck on his
head. The therapist said, 'May I help you?' The duck replied,
'Get this man off my backside!'* I've seen the same problem
take place in meetings. Either there are too many items on
the agenda or the discussion focuses on too many things.
Meetings go astray because before finalizing one point,
someone moves to the next. For example, one person talks
about when, a second person focuses on who, and a

third person asks about what. The end result is that nothing gets decided. Focus on one goal at a time.

The mind's software

Now let's turn our attention to the fact that the mind is a goal-striving mechanism and it often functions as though it were a computer in which you can access your various software packages. These software packages are based mostly upon programming which we have incorporated from role models in differing settings. We have various software packages in our minds that we use for different situations in life. These software packages are often a result of our experiences and, ultimately, of decisions we have made on a conscious and/or subconscious level. Sometimes they are simply based on history: 'That's the way my father did it;' or, 'That's the way my boss did it.' The end result is, often, that we are less effective than we could be.

Allow me to share a simple, yet telling, example of a common software package. I often say to managers, 'If you would treat your subordinates and your family as you do your customers, you'd be a big success.' When a customer has a complaint, we have a tendency to listen, understand, and communicate that we do understand. If our children have a complaint, we have a tendency to be abrupt and harsh. Why not deal with our children the way we deal with our customers? Almost any proprietor wants a customer to let him know if he or she is unhappy about anything. Why? So that the situation can be improved. What's the reason we don't use the same philosophy with our family, employees and peers? If they have a complaint, we all too frequently respond by getting defensive or offensive instead of considering their complaints as information that may be helpful to us. It is clear to me that we have a software package in our minds for communicating with employees, a different one for use with clients, still another one for supervisors, and others for spouses, children, and other significant people. Treat the important people in your life as if they were your customers.

Any time we act in an appropriate way in one situation, we can transfer that behavior to another situation. If we are understanding at work, we clearly have the ability to be understanding at home. If we are open with our friends, we can be open with our colleagues. If we are complimentary in one setting, we can be complimentary in another. If we speak in insightful and intelligent ways in one setting, we can be insightful and intelligent in another. Perhaps you and I ought to consider that we don't really need so many different software packages for different situations. Yes, it is appropriate to be flexible, to know when and how to do what you do and say what you say. *You have to stay flexible, or you'll get bent out of shape.* However, too frequently our software packages are based upon what we think other people want and expect of us. We go around trying to please and be what we think others want us to be, instead of being true to ourselves. Rabbi Mandel said, 'If I am I because I am I and you are you because you are you, then I am and you are. But if I am I because you are you, and you are you because I am I, then I'm not and you're not.'

How to plant goals in your mind

Fortunately, the conscious mind has the ability to reprogram the subconscious mind. The following paragraphs outline five specific methods which, when used mechanically and repetitively, serve to reprogram the subconscious mind. Remember that the mind is a goal-striving mechanism. When the subconscious mind believes our goals, we are likely to achieve them.

1. VISUALIZATION

Vincent Van Gogh is reputed to have said that he never painted an original painting; they were always copies of pictures in his head. George Bernard Shaw once said, 'Some people see things as they are and ask "Why?" I dream dreams that never were and ask "Why not?"'

Visualization is a formalized way of creating these pictures. However, the technique involves a great deal more than visualizing. When you use this technique, you become the director, producer and leading character of a play you create in your head. You make the play as real as possible: you see it, hear it, feel it, sense it, smell it, and even taste it, if that's appropriate. Begin by seeing and/or hearing yourself achieving your goal. Once you have accomplished that, experience (sense, feel) yourself doing or having your goal. This is a sequence that is applicable to all types of visualization techniques.

The mind processes information by the use of three channels: auditory (hearing), visual (seeing), and kinesthetic (sensing/feeling). In essence, you visualize and hear your goals and sense what it is like to achieve them. If your goal is to become a scratch golfer, for example, you can, in your mind, see, hear and sense yourself playing scratch golf, stroke for stroke. If your goal is to own a Mercedes Benz, you can see, hear and feel yourself inside the Mercedes. You smell the leather, you hear the stereo.

If you have a goal to ask for a raise, and your ultimate goal is for the other person to respond in a positive way, you may wish to create that situation in your head frequently. Athletes regularly do visualizations before participating in an event. With enough repetition, the subconscious mind will eventually believe that which you are visualizing. Once that happens, your mind strives to accomplish that goal. You are likely to behave in a manner that invites others to accommodate your vision, or to act with the direction and energy you need to achieve your goal independently.

2. SPLIT VISUALIZATION

Split visualization is like a psychological vaccination. When people receive a vaccination, dead or deactivated bacterial particles are introduced into the bloodstream.

When those particles reach the lymph nodes, the nodes create antibodies. If live bacteria of the same type ever enter the bloodstream, the antibodies are prepared for them and ready to fight them off. Split visualization accomplishes the same thing psychologically. You create the antibodies by visualizing some event in which you are about to engage. You see, hear, and feel yourself engaging in this activity, but the problem is that the person doesn't respond in the way that you desire. In fact, you imagine his responding in a negative way. The key is to see, hear and experience yourself handling the situation effectively, and coping with the negative response, even if you don't achieve your original goal. By practicing split-visualization, you are prepared for any eventuality. Equally important, now that you are prepared, you are more likely to control your anxiety and stop scaring yourself about initiating the action you have in mind.

3. AFFIRMATIONS

Affirmations are another excellent method for programming the subconscious mind to achieve your goals. It is a simple method that has been used effectively for centuries. To create an affirmation, you simply put a goal of yours into a here-and-now positive statement.

Repeat this positive statement over and over again. A well-known affirmation is 'Every day, in every way, I am getting better and better.' Another useful affirmation is, 'I am capable and lovable.' This, for example, can bring increased comfort and self-esteem as it fosters your increased capability. Remember, words do not only describe our experience, they also create it. What we say to ourselves is important. If your goal is to be more efficient, the affirmation is, 'I am an efficient person.' If you are a person who is not very receptive, you might create an affirmation like, 'The more receptive I am, the more I receive.' If you abhor problems, your affirmation might be, 'All problems are opportunities to be creative.' If you, like me, would rather be prosperous and healthy than sick and poor, your affirmation might be, 'Abundance is the natural state and I participate.'

An affirmation initially should be written down or repeated verbally at least 25 times daily. People who write down their goals usually meet them and those who don't write them down, very often do not. In the early stages of making an affirmation, it's an excellent technique to write down the affirmation and then wait quietly for a moment to sense any internal objection that may arise in opposition. If some part of you objects, write down the objection. Then write the affirmation again, and once more allow any internal objections to surface. Continue this process until the objections stop. Repeat this process daily. This is a way to get all parts of your personality, conscious and subconscious, to be in alliance and support of your goal.

I recently learned another interesting way to do affirmations. I look at the palm of my hand and state the affirmation aloud, if alone, or mentally if not. If I sense or hear an internal objection, I turn the palm of my hand over and push the objection away. Then I turn my palm up and say the affirmation again. I repeat this process until the objections stop. It is important to look at your hand and repeat the affirmations many times after the objections actually stop. Somehow, seeing your hand there seems to help. I used this method several years ago to lose twelve pounds. I said, 'I eat nutritious food in reasonable quantities.' After losing weight and gaining it back many times, I lost the twelve pounds and have kept them off. Continue the affirmation when you need support. For me, it was before a buffet supper.

Affirmations should not be tentative. They should be positive and in the present tense. If it raises too many objections at first to say, 'I am an excellent communicator,' for example, you can begin by saying, 'I am becoming more communicative.' After all your states of mind agree with that, you can progress to 'I am an excellent communicator.'

Affirmations are good to use in times of stress. With time, your subconscious mind will believe the affirmation. You are then likely to get creative ideas or seize the opportunities to make it happen.

One key issue with affirmations, as well as with visualizations, is that it is important to behave as if the goal has already been accomplished. This is part of the process of conditioning your subconscious mind to accept the reality of your desired situation.

4. PICTURES AND GOAL CARDS

Continuing the process of programming your subconscious mind involves having actual photographs of yourself, e.g. in front of a plane, sitting in a Mercedes. If you want to lose extra weight, you might find an old photo of yourself in a swimsuit when you looked the way you would now like to look. I have a friend who had himself photographed standing in front of an expensive plane. He now owns that plane. The idea behind all this is simple: every time you see yourself having something, or doing something, this stimulates the cells of recognition in your brain, and continues that important process of stimulating your subconscious mind to believe and to work towards your goals.

Another useful technique is to write down a clear description of your goals, including all important elements, e.g. what the goal looks like, sounds like, and feels like. If my goal is to own a beautiful house by a river in the mountains, first I would see, hear, and sense as much of the scene as I could. For example, I see a brick home with wood shingles, a huge oak door, and vaulted ceilings inside. I see the river, the beautiful evergreen trees and lots of birds. What does it sound like to me? I hear the sound of wind rushing through the trees and I can hear the raging river. I can also hear the wonderful silence of being in an isolated area. What do I sense? I feel the fresh air on my face. As I walk through the house, I feel the thick carpet between my toes. I feel a sense of relaxation. I can even smell the wooden floor. I would then thoroughly write out this description on a goal card, and keep it handy (in my wallet or on my refrigerator) so that I could see and touch it frequently. Every time I look at the goal card or touch it, I stimulate my subconscious mind, my creative energies, and my conscious mind to secure ways of owning that house. Some of my business clients have had success with this technique. One of the managers I consulted with wanted to become a more outgoing person. He wrote down what he would look and sound like, as well as how he would feel. Within months, he experienced himself to be as he envisioned — a more comfortable and outgoing person.

5. RETURN TO SUCCESSFUL EXPERIENCES

This technique is used when you are at a plateau, or feeling as if you're on a losing streak. Very often, a negative momentum works in the same way as a positive momentum. You might have failed to close the last two sales and are starting to feel down. You are in a losing frame of mind. When you start to plateau or slide back, you need to return to successful experiences. To do this, you visualize a recent experience at which you were very successful. If there isn't a recent experience, a more distant one will do. In this exercise, you see, hear, and sense the experience as completely as possible, so that you can stimulate that winning feeling again and get a positive momentum going. Again, all these techniques help in the process of programming the subconscious mind to believe. Remember,

> when the subconscious mind believes it, you are likely to achieve it.

Use structure and strokes for goal accomplishment

Each person has different components within his personality. This is why you can be 'of two minds' about something; why you can carry on a dialogue in your head and one reason why you experience internal conflict. Transactional Analysis is a field of psychology and a communication method. One aspect of T.A. describes these personality parts and their interactions, and defines how to use them to our advantage. (You can learn more about Transactional Analysis from my earlier book, *The Transactional Manager.*) One state of the conscious mind is the Natural Child. This is the state that experiences needs, wants, and expresses feelings and desires. We have both biological and psychological needs. A need is something we must have in order to exist, without which we will either die or become mentally unstable. Examples of biological needs are the need for air and the need for water. Two psychological needs of the Natural Child are 'structure' and 'strokes'.

You and I have a strong need for structure, that is, a need to know who, what, when, where, how and why. We have a need for some semblance of organization and order in our lives. This need for definition is clearly exemplified when we feel quite uncomfortable because we don't have these questions answered — on a new job, or after moving to a new city, or when starting a new relationship. We all want to know how to do something, and what is expected of us. We don't relax until we get these questions answered. As soon as the structure of a situation is defined, we tend to feel much more comfortable. Think of a simple example of moving from one house to another: the discomfort you feel until you have put things away, know your way around the neighborhood, and so on.

When you want to make a change, it's important to provide a structure for that change. It is difficult, for example, to lose weight or get in shape when you do it in a haphazard way. It becomes real after you have established a structure or routine.

A 'stroke' is a unit of attention — any kind of attention. If for some reason no one pays verbal or non-verbal attention to us, we begin to sense a stroke hunger, a need for contact with another living being. This is why the hermit is such a rare person — and even the hermit usually gets strokes from contact with animals. Human beings need the strokes we provide for one another. Without strokes, most of us soon become uncomfortable. If we have too few strokes for too long, we tend to get sick, or we may even develop emotional illness. Most of us will therefore go to great lengths to get the strokes we need. If we can't get positive attention, we'll make do with negative attention. Either way, a stroke is a stroke, and strokes are what we need.

Whatever you stroke, continues; whatever you ignore, diminishes significantly. This means that paying attention to specific behavior, either positively or negatively, invites the behavior to continue. On the other hand, when we ignore it, that behavior disappears. Have you ever noticed that there's a certain employee you stroke only negatively, and rarely, if ever, stroke positively? When she does what she's supposed to do, you pay little or no attention to her. *This is referred to as 'Seagull Management'. The manager/parent comes flying in, makes a lot of noise, messes on people and flies out.* The quiet child in the classroom tends to be ignored; the very bright child, good–looking child, slow child, or very disruptive child tends to get a lot of strokes.

[handwritten margin note: reward positive behavior]

STRUCTURE AND STROKES, WHEN COMBINED, ARE A POWERFUL TEAM FOR THE ACCOMPLISHMENT OF A GOAL

Likewise, these are the two primary elements which are needed to institute a new idea, a new policy, a new product, an exercise program, or any individual endeavor that you undertake. How well organizations such as Alcoholics Anonymous and Weight Watchers have capitalized on this idea! The two key ingredients in both programs are structure and strokes. A primary reason these organizations are successful is that they meet these two very basic human needs. Some aspects of the structure of Weight Watchers are recipes, behavior modification ideas, weighing food, and weighing-in. When people weigh-in, they stand up; announce their achievement; and receive verbal and non-verbal praise. The wonderful strokes that a person receives when someone says, 'Gosh, you look great !' help it to be worthwhile. Alcoholics Anonymous has the same aspects of structure and strokes: The Twelve Steps, the regular meetings, the availability of someone to contact. Standing up at the weekly meeting, having that someone available, the terrific strokes from fellow members, all help to ensure that members get the strokes they need.

Whenever you wish to accomplish something, or whenever you change from one situation to another (a job, a relationship, a position, a city), the faster you get 'who, what, when, where, how and why' defined and instituted, and the faster you develop your sources of stroking, the faster you will adjust. When you're in a business meeting and somebody comes up with a good idea, that idea will die if you allow it to be poorly defined. It will live if you give it structure and strokes. For example, 'That's a good idea, Tom. What kind of help do you need to implement it? Who do you want to talk to? When will you meet? What kind of budget do you need? Let's develop a timetable.' Follow-up is needed as well. This will probably include regular communication with the person, and pats on the back when appropriate. If you're promoted to a new job, to get the needed structure, ask for job descriptions, personnel codes, lines-of-authority charts, rules and regulations, adequate time with supervisors in the early stages, training, and appropriate support.

To accomplish goals, especially long-term goals, structure and strokes are absolute necessities. Once goals are clearly defined, the next step is to determine the activities that will be needed to accomplish them. Activities and their specifics are forms of structure. Without periodic reinforcement from others, it becomes difficult to stay motivated for the long-term goal.

3 treat yourself and others with dignity and respect

Self-love is the key

Everyone has inherent worth and dignity. Your actions speak of your commitment to this concept. It is important for your communication to reflect the fact that you, and others, deserve to be treated with dignity and respect.

When I say that everyone has inherent worth and dignity, I mean that this applies to you, also. The old saying that 'you have to love yourself' may seem hackneyed, but I believe it's true. People who feel good about themselves produce good results. Having respect for yourself and caring about yourself are the foundations for your ability to deal with others effectively.

My philosophy is that if you don't like yourself, you have bad taste. Obviously, I'm talking about liking yourself as a person. You may not like your own behavior at times. If your behavior doesn't get you the results you want, change it. You can dislike some of your behavior without rejecting everything about yourself.

The same goes for me: if you don't like me, you have bad taste. You may not like all the things I do. Although I'm okay, that doesn't necessarily mean that my behavior is always okay. *As is true of all people, I am resistible at times. There is no doubt that you can have forgettable experiences with me, and that you will sometimes find me underwhelming. (In fact, a woman recently told me that I was extinguished-looking.)* Nevertheless, you can separate me from my behavior, and like me as a human being. I must add that if I engage in a lot of negative behavior, people may feel quite justified in rejecting me on this ground. In the vast majority of cases, however, a person's behavior is not so negative that I would reject them outright.

Even when you experience a strong dislike for someone, it is almost always the person's behavior that you dislike — something he does or doesn't do, or the way he does it. Perhaps you perceive his behavior as extremely objectionable. You certainly don't have to like such behavior. Would you be willing to have someone whose behavior you dislike punished in a corporal manner, or to have them sent to jail, without due process of law? I hope not. Regardless of their behavior, humans do have inherent worth and dignity.

CHILDHOOD DECISIONS ABOUT OURSELVES AND OTHERS

All of us have made important and basic decisions about ourselves. As youngsters, we decided that we're either 'okay' or 'not – okay,' depending upon whether our needs and wants were met effectively. We decided either 'I'm okay and you're okay,' or 'I'm not – okay and you're not – okay.' The latter decision is often manifested as 'I'm okay and you're not,' or 'I'm not – okay, you are,' but these positions are a cover-up for a basic 'I'm not – okay and you're not – okay' decision. Under stress, this early decision may resurface and have a profound effect on our attitudes and actions. One way to get in touch with your basic position is to note your behavior during conflict. One of these unfortunate positions may manifest itself, or you may realize that you maintain your own sense of self-worth and the worth of others even under difficult circumstances. If you don't maintain this sense of self-respect, you can learn to do so. Your basic position can be changed, because it is based upon your own decisions.

People often say, 'Certainly it's okay to say I love myself, but it's not easy to do.' I agree. I advise those people to behave in ways that are indicative of self-respect and respect for others. These '**Say It Straight**' guidelines will invite others to respond to you in kind. When you are receiving those kinds of responses from others, you will feel okay about yourself. In other words, behave in okay ways and you'll feel okay about yourself.

SELFLESSNESS AND SELFISHNESS ARE NOT VIRTUES

A great driving force in people is the desire to feel important. Unfortunately, many societal groups tend to invite people into selflessness, which amounts to giving up their sense of self-importance. Selflessness is no more a virtue than selfishness. If you don't charge your own battery, you don't have energy for others.

I view selfishness as a defense. Frequently, 'selfish people' started to focus predominantly on themselves in early childhood when many of their wants were rejected: 'If I don't look out for Number One, then nobody will because nobody really cares about me.' In other cases, some parents lead their children to believe that the world revolves around the youngsters' needs and wants and no one else's. An 'I'm okay, you're okay' position requires the belief that we both count. The needs and wants of both of us are important. **It's not me or you; it's me and you.**

The motivation for selfishness, as with many other ineffective attitudes, is okay. The behavior isn't. When a person takes a 'me first' attitude, it is often to protect himself and to make sure that his needs are met. I won't fault his desire to be taken care of. His method is often questionable, but his intention is positive. Now that I have learned to separate people's intentions from their behavior, I find it much easier to treat them with dignity and respect.

People who are being selfless often had a parent who

modelled selflessness. That parent put the needs and wants of the children, spouse, and others first, and discounted his or her own needs and wants. Children often then believe that they must be the same way in order to get their parents' approval. Another possibility is that a child decided that her needs didn't count because she was rejected for having wants or needs.

Treating people with respect includes confrontation. If someone's behavior is harmful to himself or to others, to confront it is a caring act. If the person is putting himself down, or treating me unfairly, it is incumbent upon me to speak up. Sometimes a constructive expression of anger is in order to communicate the strength of my feelings and caring so that I am believed. I also feel relieved by my expression of feelings.

Actually, treating yourself and others with dignity and respect is the only principle that is needed for effective human relations. It covers all the others to be presented. Rabbi Hillel is quoted as saying, 'Do not do unto others what is hateful to you.' Many people, however, do not know how to consistently treat themselves and others with respect. This book deals with the how-to's of carrying out this principle.